आ नो भद्राः क्रतवो यन्तु विश्वतः

Let noble thoughts come to us from every side

—Rigveda, I-89-i

BHAVAN'S BOOK UNIVERSITY

SANDHYAVANDANAM

by

P. SESHADRI

BHAVAN'S BOOK UNIVERSITY

SANDHYAVANDANAM

P. SESHADRI

2023
BHARATIYA VIDYA BHAVAN
Kulapati K. M. Munshi Marg
Mumbai - 400007

First Edition	-	*1974*
Second Edition	-	*1978*
Third Edition	-	*1987*
Fourth Edition	-	*1989*
Fifth Edition	-	*1995*
Sixth Editon	-	*1996*
Seventh Edition	-	*1998*
Eighth Edition	-	*2000*
Nineth Edition	-	*2003*
Tenth Edition	-	*2006*
Eleventh Edition	-	*2013*
Twelveth Edition	-	*2023*

Price : ₹ 90/-

PRINTED IN INDIA
By Atul Goradia at Siddhi Printers, 13/14, Bhabha Building,
13th Khetwadi Lane, Mumbai - 400004, and
Published by P. V. Sankarankutty, Director,
for the Bharatiya Vidya Bhavan,
Kulapati Munshi Marg, Mumbai - 400007
E-mail : publications@bhavans.info
Web-site : www.bhavans.info

KULAPATI'S FREFACE

THE Bharatiya Vidya Bhavan—that Institute of Indian Culture in Bombay—needed a Book University, a series of books which, if read, would serve the purpose of providing higher education. Particular emphasis, however, was to be put on such literature as revealed the deeper impulsions of India. As a first step, it was decided to bring out in English 100 books, 50 of which were to be taken in hand almost at once. Each book was to contain from 200 to 250 pages.

It is our intention to publish the books we select, not only in English, but also in the following Indian languages: Hindi, Bengali, Gujarati, Marathi, Tamil, Telugu, Kannada and Malayalam.

This scheme, involving the publication of 900 volumes, requires ample funds and an all-India organisation. The Bhavan is exerting its utmost to supply them.

The objectives for which the Bhavan stands are the reintegration of the Indian culture in the light of modern knowledge and to suit our present-day needs and the resuscitation of its fundamental values in their pristine vigour.

Let me make our goal more explicit:

We seek the dignity of man, which necessarily implies the creation of social conditions which would allow him freedom to evolve along the lines of his own temperament and capacities; we seek the harmony of individual efforts and social relations, not in any makeshift way, but within the frame-work of the Moral Order; we seek the creative art of life; by the alchemy of which human limitations are progressively transmuted, so that man may become the instrument of God, and is able to see Him in all and all in Him.

The world, we feel, is too much with us. Nothing would uplift or inspire us so much as the beauty and aspiration which such books can teach.

In this series, therefore, the literature of India, ancient and modern, will be published in a form easily accessible to all. Books in other literatures of the world, if they illustrate the principles we stand for, will also be included.

This common pool of literature, it is hoped, will enable the reader, eastern or western, to understand and appreciate currents of world thought, as also the movements of the mind in India, which, though they flow through different linguistic channels, have a common urge and aspiration.

Fittingly, the Book University's first venture is the *Mahabharata*, summarised by one of the greatest living Indians, C. Rajagopalachari; the second work is on a section of it, the *Gita* by H. V. Divatia, an eminent jurist and a student of philosophy. Centuries ago, it was proclaimed of the *Mahabharata*: "What is not in it, is nowhere." After twenty-five centuries, we can use the same words about it. He who knows it not, knows not the heights and depths of the soul; he misses the trials and tragedy and the beauty and grandeur of life.

The *Mahabharata* is not a mere epic; it is a romance, telling the tale of heroic men and women and of some who were divine; it is a whole literature in itself, containing a code of life, a philosophy of social and ethical relations, and speculative thought on human problems that is hard to rival; but, above all, it has for its core the *Gita*, which is, as the world is beginning to find out, the noblest of scriptures and the grandest of sagas in which the climax is reached in the wondrous Apocalypse in the Eleventh Canto.

Through such books alone the harmonies underlying true culture, I am convinced, will one day reconcile the disorders of modern life.

I thank all those who have helped to make this new branch of the Bhavan's activity successful.

1, QUEEN VICTORIA ROAD,
NEW DELHI:
3rd October, 1951.

K. M. Munshi

ACHAMANAM

अच्युताय नमः *Achyutaya namah*
अनन्ताय नमः *Anantaya namah*
गोविन्दाय नमः *Govindaya namah*

Achamanam, that is, sipping of the water with the above mantras, one sipping for each mantra, will remove all the ills of the body and mind. This is called *Namatrayividya* or the worship with the three names which will cure all diseases, physical and mental. There is a well-known sloka to the effect that the medicine constituting the repetition of the three names of the Lord अच्युत (*Achyuta*), अनन्त (*Ananta*) and गोविन्द (*Govinda*) will certainly cure all diseases.

The *Achamanam* must be performed facing the east or north. It should not be done facing the west or south. Leaving out the thumb and the forefinger, the other three fingers must be bent a little and then a small space for keeping is found in the inner hand. Water should be poured there and sipped thrice uttering the three mantras in succession. Then the hand should be washed twice. If there is *pavitra* in the second finger, it should be removed at the time of *Achamana* and worn again after *Achamana.*

The following twelve names of the Lord should thereafter be uttered, touching each limb of the body with the particular finger mentioned below. This signifies that all the senses are dedicated to the service of God.

When the senses are made introspective instead of going outwards to the external objects, the natural bliss of the soul will be manifested. The names are —
केशव । नारायण । माधव । गोविन्द । विष्णु । मधुसूदन । त्रिविक्रम । वामन । श्रीधर । हृषीकेश । पद्मनाभ । दामोदर ।

Kesava/ Narayana/ Madhava /Govinda / Vishnu / Madhusoodhana / Trivikrama / Vamana / Sridhara / Hrishikesa Padmanabha / Damodara /'

As the thumb and the mouth are the seats of fire, the names केशव (*Kesava*) and नारायण (*Narayana*) are uttered with the thumb touching the right and left cheeks respectively. The second finger and the eyes are regarded as the seats of the sun and so with the second finger the right and left eyes are touched, repeating the names माधव (*Madhava*) and गोविन्द (*Govinda*). The forefinger and the nose, being considered as seats of Vayu (wind) the right and left parts of the nose are touched by the forefinger with the names विष्णु (*Vishnu*) and मधुसूदन (*Madhusoodana*) being repeated respectively. The little finger and the ears are seats of *Indra* and hence by the little finger the right and left ears are touched uttering the names त्रिविक्रम (*Trivikrama*) and वामन (*Vamana*) respectively. As the middle finger and the shoulder are regarded as the seats of *Prajapati*, that finger should touch the shoulders, when the person utters the names श्रीधर (*Sridhara*) and हृषीकेश (*Hrishikesa*) respectively. The inner part of the hand and the heart being considered as the seats of *Paramatma* the inner hand should touch the heart and top of the head, uttering the names पद्मनाभ (*Padmanabha*) and दामोदर (*Damodara*) in succession.

Thus all the parts of the body are protected by repeating the names of God.

Afterwards, the Lord Ganapati is meditated to ward off all hindrances :—

शुक्लाम्बरधरं विष्णुं शशिवर्णं चतुर्भुजम् ।
प्रसन्नवदनं ध्यायेत् सर्वविघ्नोपशान्तये ॥

Shuklambaradharam Vishnum shashivarnam chaturbhujam
Prasannavadanam dhyayet sarvavighnopasantaye.

The two hands should be folded and the two sides of the forehead struck gently five times, repeating the above mantra, with the meditation of Ganapati and imagining that the nectar collected in the head according to the Yogasastras is entering into each nerve.

Meaning

विष्णुं (*Vishnum*)	— All-pervading
शुक्लाम्बरधरं (*Shuklambaradharam*)	— Wearing a white garment
शशिवर्णं (*Shashivarnam*)	— Shining like the moon
चतुर्भुजं (*Chaturbhujam*)	— having four hands

प्रसन्नवदनं (*Prasannavadanam*) — having a cheerful face
सर्वविघ्नोपशान्तये (*Sarvavighno-pasantaye*) — to ward off all obstacles
ध्यायेत् (*Dhyayet*) — should be meditated.

The All-pervading, clad in white garment, resplendent like the Moon, the four-armed and the cheerful-faced Lord should be meditated to ward off all obstacles.

PRANAYAMA

Next comes *Pranayama* i. e. Control of Prana.

ओं भूः । ओं भुवः । ओँ सुवः । ओं महः । ओं जनः । ओं तपः । ओँ सत्यं । ओं तत् सवितुर्वरेण्यं भर्गो देवस्य धीमहि । धियो यो नः प्रचोदयात् । ओमापो ज्योती-रसोऽमृतं ब्रह्म भूर्भुवस्सुवरोम् ।

Om Bhuh / Om Bhuvah / Om Suvaha / Om Mahah / Om Janah / Om Tapah / Om Satyam / Om Tat Saviturvarenyam Bhargo Devasya Dhimahi / Dhiyo yo Nah Prachodayat / Om Apo Jyoti-rasomritam Brahma Bhurbhuvassuvarom.

The forefinger and the middle finger should be bent and by the thumb and second finger, the nose must be touched on either side, the right nostril should be closed and air must be taken slowly by the left nostril and then that should be closed and after a time the air slowly sent out by the right nostril. The inhaling is called *Puraka*, the retaining *Kumbhaka* and the exhaling *Rechaka*. The proportion of time of these three viz. *Puraka, Kumbhaka* and *Rechaka* should be in the ratio 1 : 3: 2. The *Puraka, Kumbhaka* and *Rechaka* all three together, make one *Pranayama*. From ओं भूः (*Om*

Bhuh) upto धियो यो नः प्रचोदयात् (*Dhiyo yo nah prachodayat*) would be *Puraka*. From ओमापो ज्योती-रसोऽमृतं ब्रह्म भूर्भुवस्सुवरोम् (*Omapo Jyoti-rasomritam Brahma Bhurbhuvassuvarom*) upto ओं भूः ओं भुवः (*Om Bhuh, Om Bhuvah*) will be one *Kumbhaka*. The third turn from ओं भूः (*Om Bhuh*) upto the end will be *Rechaka*.

Meaning

ओं भूः *Om Bhuh* — The omkar is this world
ओं भुवः *Om Bhuvah* — The Om is the world Bhuvah
ओं सुवः *Om Suvah* — The Om is the world Suvah
ओं महः *Om Mahah* — The Om is the world Maha
ओं जनः *Om Janah* — The Om is the world Jana
ओं तपः *Om Tapah* — The Om is the world Tapa
ओं सत्यं *Om Satyam* — The Om is the world Satya
ओं यः *Om Yah* — He who is the Supreme sel'
नः *Nah* — Our
धियः *Dhiyah* — Intellect
प्रचोदयात् *Prachodayat* — Inspires
तत् *Tat* — That
सवितुः *Savituh* — Creator's
देवस्य *Devasya* — The Lord's
वरेण्यं *Varenyam* — Most Excellent
भर्गः *Bhargah* — Light
धीमहि *Dhimahi* — We meditate
ओं *Om* — The Om
आपः *Apah* — Water
ज्योतिः *Jyotih* — Light
रसः *Rasah* — The earth and the Air
अमृतं *Amritam* — Eternal
ब्रह्म *Brahma* — The all-pervading sky
भूर्भुवस्सुवरोम् *Bhurbhuvas-suvarom* — The mind, the intellect and the egoism are also that Om.

The Seven worlds beginning with this universe भूः *Bhuh* are verily the Omkar. He, the Supreme Lord, inspires our intellects. We meditate on the light of the Creator of the Worlds. Water, light, this world, air and the sky as well as the mind, the intellect and the egoism are also that Om.

Sankalpah: ममोपात्त समस्त–दुरित क्षय–द्वारा–श्री–परमेश्वर प्रीत्यर्थं प्रातः सन्ध्याम् उपासिष्ये *Mamopatta-Samasta Duritakshaya -dwara-Sri - Parameswara - preetyartham Pratah Sandhya-mupasishye.*

माध्यान्हिकं करिष्ये ॥ *Madhyanhikam Karishye*
सायं सन्ध्यामुपासिष्ये ॥ *Sayam Sandhyamupasishye.*

The Sankalpa should be made after *Pranayama* and then alone any work should be begun. When the Mantra is recited, the left hand should be below the right hand and both hands clasped and placed on the thigh.

ममोपात्त *Mamopatta*	—	All that has accrued in me
समस्त–दुरित *Samasta-durita*		All sins
क्षय–द्वारा *Kshaya-dwara*	—	By destroying
श्री परमेश्वर-प्रीत्यर्थं *Sri Parameswara Preetyartham*	—	to be worthy of the Grace of the Supreme Lord
प्रातः *Pratah*	—	of the morning
सन्ध्याम् *Sandhyam*	—	the Sandhya Goddess
उपासिष्ये *Upasishye*	—	I begin to worship.

I worship the Sandhya Goddess of the morning to be worthy of the Grace of the Supreme Lord by the destruction of all sins that have accumulated in me in previous births.

MARJANAM

मार्जनम्

आपो हिष्ठा मयो भुवः। ता न ऊर्जे दधातन। महे रणाय चक्षसे। यो वः शिवतमो रसः। तस्य भाजयतेह नः। उशतीरिव मातरः। तस्मा अरंगमाम वः। यस्य क्षयाय जिन्वथ। आपो जनयथा च नः। ओं भूर्भुवस्सुवः।

Apohishta mayo bhuvah / ta na oorje dadhatana / mahe ranaya chakshase / yo vah sivatamorasah / Tasya bhajayateha nah / Usateeriya Matarah / Tasma arangamama vah / yasya kṣhayaya jinvatha / Apo janayatha cha nah / Om Bhurbhuvas-suvah.

With the second finger of the right hand write the letter *Om* on water and uttering the word श्रीकेशवाय नमः *Srį kesavaya namah* touch the centre of the brows with that very finger.

With the first seven mantras sprinkle water on the head with the second finger. Reciting the eighth Mantra touch the feet with the second finger. Reciting the ninth mantra sprinkle water again on the head. Then repeating the mantra *Om Bhurbhuvassuvah* ओं भूर्भुवस्सुवः make a circuit of your head.

Meaning :

ओं श्रीकेशवाय नमः *Om Sri Kesavaya namah* — Prostration to Sri Kesava

आपः *Apah* — Goddesses of waters

मयो भुवः *Mayo bhuvah* — be the cause of conferring the highest bliss

ष्ठा हि *Shta hi* — are verily

ताः *Tah* — Such Goddesses as you

नः *Nah* — to us
महे *Mahe* — Great
रणाय *Ranaya* — Beautiful
चक्षसे *Chakshase* — for the eye of knowledge
ऊर्जे *Oorje* — Nourishment
दधातन *Dadhatana* — Give
वः *Vah* — of you
यः *Yah* — that
शिवतमः *Sivatamah* — most auspicious
रसः *Rasah* — bliss
तस्य *Tasya* — for that
इह *Iha* — herc
नः *Nah* — us
उशतीः *Usatih* — Loving .
मातरः इव *Matarah Iva* — Like mothers
भाजयतेह *Bhajayateha* — make us worthy
यस्य क्षयाय *yasya kshayaya* — for establishing that bĺiss
जिन्वथ *Jinvatha* — you shine with love
तस्मा *Tasma* — for that bliss
वः *Vah* — you
अरम् *Aram* — with great eagerness
गमाम: *Gamamah* — we go in for
आपः *Apah* — water goddesses
नः *Nah* — us
जनयथा *Janayatha* — making us purc by knowledge, give us rebirth.

Om-prostration to Sri Kesava. You water Goddesses are the causes of conferring the highest happiness. Even suech are you. Give us nourishment for the eye of knowledge whkch is so great and beautiful. The most auspicious Bliss that is in you, be like loving mothers to give us that Supreme

Bliss. You are love personified and the seat of that Bliss. We pray you with great earnestness to give us that Bliss. Make us pure by knowledge and be reborn as it were resplendently.

प्रातः *Pratah* प्राशनम् (*Prasanam*)

सूर्यश्च मा मन्युश्च मन्युपतयश्च मन्युकृतेभ्यः। पापेभ्यो रक्षन्ताम्। यद्रात्रिया पापमकार्षम्। मनसा वाचा हस्ताभ्याम्। पद्भ्यामुदरेण शिश्ना॥ रात्रिस्तदवलुम्पतु। यत् किंच दुरितं मयि इदमहं माममृतयोनौ। सूर्ये ज्योतिषि जुहोमि स्वाहा॥

Suryascha ma manyuscha manyupatayascha manyukritebhyah / Papebhyo rakshantam / Yadratriya papamakarsham / Manasa vacha hasthabhyam / Padbhyamudarena sisna / Ratristadavalumpatu / Yat kimcha duritam mayi idamaham mamamritayonau / Surye Jyotishi Juhomi Swaha //

Reciting this mantra, take water in your right hand measuring a full sized hollow of the palm and drink it.

Meaning

सूर्यश्च *Suryascha*	—	The Sun
मन्युश्च *Manyuscha*	—	and anger
मन्युपतयश्च *Manyupa tayascha*	—	and the God of anger
मन्युकृतेभ्यः *Manyu-kritebhyah*	—	all actions done by anger
पापेभ्यः *Papebhyah*	—	from sins.
मा *ma*	—	me
रक्षन्ताम् *Rakshantam*	—	protect

रात्रिया *Ratriya*	—	all night
मनसा *Manasa*	—	by the mind
वाचा *Vacha*	—	by speech
हस्ताभ्याम् *Hastabhyam*	—	by the two hands
पद्भ्याम् *Padbhyam*	—	by the two feet
उदरेण *Udarena*	—	by the stomach
शिश्ना *Sishna*	—	by the sexual organ
किंच *Kincha*	—	and also
मयि *Mayi*	—	in me
यत् *Yat*	—	that
दुरितं *duritam*	—	sin
तत् *Tat*	—	that
रात्रि *Ratri*	—	the presiding deity of night
अवलुम्पतु *Avalumpatu*	—	may remove
इदम् माम् *Idam Mam*	—	this sin being removed from me
अहं *Aham*	—	I
अमृत-योनौ *Amrita-yonau*	—	the cause of moksha
सूर्ये ज्योतिषि *Surye Jyotishi*	—	In the supreme Lord in Sun
	—	of Supreme light
जुहोमि *Juhomi*	—	sacrifice
स्वाहा *Swaha*	—	Let it be well done.

Save me from the sins born of anger, O Lord! The Sun, anger and Anger God, what has been done at night by the mind, speech, the two hands, two feet, the stomach and sexual organ as well as all other sins attaching to me may be removed.

Thus I, freed from all sins offer oblations to the Supreme Lord, the Supreme Light in the form of the Sun so that I may be worthy of moksha.

मध्याह्ने *Madhyanhe* : (Noon)—

आपः पुनन्तु पृथिवीं पृथिवी पूता पुनातु माम् । पुनन्तु ब्रह्मणस्पतिर्ब्रह्म पूता पुनातु माम् ॥ यदुच्छिष्टमभोज्यं यद्वा दुश्चरितं मम । सर्वं पुनन्तु मामापोऽसतां च प्रतिग्रहँ स्वाहा ॥

Apah punantu prithivim prithivi puta punatu mam / Punantu Brahmanaspatirbrahma puta punatu mam / yaduchhishtam abhojyam yadva duscharitam mama / Sarvam punantu mamaposatam cha pratigrahagg swaha.

This is to be recited at noon and water sipped afterward.

Meaning

आपः *Apah*	—	the deity of water
पृथिवीम् *Prithivim*	—	the earth
पुनन्तु *Punantu*	—	may purify
पूता *Puta*	—	thus purified
पृथिवी *Prithivi*	—	the earth
माम् *Mam*	—	me
पुनातु *Punatu*	—	purify
ब्रह्मणस्पतिः *Brahmanaspatih*	—	Teacher who is the repository of Vedas.
पुनन्तु *Punantu*	—	may purify
पूता *Puta*	—	the ever pure
ब्रह्म *Brahma*	—	the veda
माम् *Mam*	—	me
पुनातु *Punatu*	—	may purify
उच्छिष्टम् *Ucchhishtam*	—	the remnant of food taken by another
अभोज्यम् *Abhojyam*	—	Uneatable food

यत् *Yat*	—	that
मया *Maya*	—	by me
वा *va*	—	or
मम *Mama*	—	My
यत् *Yat*	—	that
दुश्चरितं *Duscharitam*	—	bad conduct
किंच *Kincha*	—	and also
असतां *Asatam*	—	from the bad people
प्रतिग्रहँ *Praitigrahagg*	—	the gift
सर्वं *Sarvam*	—	from all
माम् *Mam*	—	me
पुनन्तु *Punantu*	—	may purify
स्वाहा *Swaha*	—	I offer myself to the blaze of Paramatman

May the Goddess of water purify the earth. May that purified earth purify me and the teacher of Vedas. May the ever purified Vedas purify me. The remnant of another's food or uneatable food which I have eaten and my bad conduct and the gifts I have received from bad people, may I be purified from all that. I offer myself to be consumed at the blaze of the Supreme Being.

सायंकाले *Sayamkale* (Evening) :

अग्निश्च मा मन्युश्च मन्युपतयश्च मन्युकृतेभ्यः। पापेभ्यो रक्षन्ताम्। यदन्हा पापमकार्षम्। मनसा वाचा हस्ताभ्याम्। पद्भ्यामुदरेण शिश्ना। अहस्तदवलुम्पतु। यत् किंच दुरितं मयि। इदमहं माममृतयोनौ। सत्ये ज्योतिषि जुहोमि स्वाहा।

Agnischa ma manyuscha manyupatayascha manyukritebhyah / Papebhyo rakshantam / yadanha papamakarsham / Manasa Vacha hastabhyam / Padbhyam Udarena Sishna / Ahasta-

davalumpatu | Yat kincha duritam mayi | Idamaham mamrita-yonau Satye jyotishi juhomi swaha.

This is to be recited in the evening and water sipped.

Meaning

अग्नि: *Agnih*	—	The Lord of Fire
मन्युश्च *Manyuscha*	—	and anger
मन्युपतयश्च *Manyupatayascha*	—	and Lord of Anger
मन्युकृतेभ्य: पापेभ्य: *Manyukrite-bhyah Papebhyah*	—	From the sins committed by anger
मा *ma*	—	me
रक्षन्ताम् *Rakshantam*	—	protect
अह्ना *Anha*	—	in the day
मनसा *Manasa*	—	by the mind
वाचा *Vacha*	—	by words
हस्ताभ्याम् *Hastabhyam*	—	by the two hands
पद्भ्याम् *Padbhyam*	—	by the two feet
उदरेण *Udarena*	—	by the stomach
शिश्ना *Sishna*	—	by the sexual organ
यत् पापम् *Yat-papam*	—	that sin
अकार्षम् *Akarsham*	—	has been done by me
किंच *Kincha*	—	and also
यत् दुरितं *Yat-duritam*	—	whatever sin
तत् *Tat*	—	that
अह: *Ahah*	—	The lord of Day
अवलुम्पतु *Avalumpatu*	—	May remove
इदम् मां *Idam Mam*	—	Thus me purified of all sins
अहं *Aham*	—	I
अमृतयोनौ *Amritayonau*	—	the cause of Moksha
सत्ये ज्योतिषि *Satye Jyothishi*	—	The blaze of eternal truth

'जुहोमि *Juhomi*	—	I offer as an oblation
स्वाहा *Swaha*	—	Let this homa be well performed.

May the Lord of Fire, anger, and God of anger protect me from all the sins committed by anger. May that sin done by me during the course of the day by the mind, word, the two hands, the two feet, the stomach and the sexual organ be removed by the deity of the day. Thus purified I offer myself as an oblation to the resplendent Supreme light, the cause of Moksha.

आचमनम् (*Achamanam*) पुनर्मार्जनम् (*Punarmarjanam*) मार्जनम् (*Marjanam*).

दधिक्राविण्णो अकारिषं जिष्णोरश्वस्य वाजिनः । सुरभि नो मुखा करत् प्रण आयूंषि तारिषत् ॥ आपो हि ष्ठा मयोभुवः । ता न ऊर्जे दधातन । महे रणाय चक्षसे । यो वः शिवतमो रसः । तस्य भाजयतेह नः । उशतीरिव मातरः । तस्मा अरंगमाम वः । यस्य क्षयाय जिन्वथ । आपो जनयथा च नः । ओं भूर्भुवस्सुवः

Dadhikravinno akarisham jishnorasvasya vajinah / Surabhi no mukha karat Prana Ayoogumshi tarishat

Apo hi shta mayo bhuvah / Ta na oorjhe dadhatana / Mahe ranaya chakshase / Yo vah sivatamo rasah / Tasya bhajhayateha nah / Usatiriva Matarah / Tasma arangamama vah Yasya kshayaya jinvatha / Apo janayatha cha nah / Om Bhurbhuvassuvah.

By the first mantra beginning with दधिक्राविण्णो (*Dadhikravinno*) and by the seven mantras beginning with आपो हि ष्ठा (*Apo hi shta*) water should be sprinkled on the head.

Uttering the next mantra the feet should be touched and finally reciting आपो जनयथा च नः (*Apo janayatha cha nah*) the water should be thrown round the head.

Meaning

दधिक्राविष्णो *Dadhikra-vinno*	—	The Lord who supports, rules and measures all the worlds
जिष्णोः *Jishnoh*	—	The victorious
अश्वस्य *Asvasya*	—	The hayagriva form, the seat of all knowledge
वाजिनः *Vajinah*	—	The swiftest, supreme Lord
अकारिषं *Akarisham*	—	I worship
नः *Na*	—	our
मुखा *Mukha*	—	face and other senses
सुरभि *Surabhi*	—	doing good
करत् *Karat*	—	may make
आयूंषि *Ayoogumshi*	—	The Life
तारिषत् *tarishat*	—	Be without any hindrance
आपो हिष्ठा *Apo hishta*	—	etc. as commented before

May the Lord, the Supporter, the Ruler and the Measurer of all the worlds, the Victorious, the Seat of all knowledge Who has taken the form of *hayagriva*, the Swift Supreme Lord, whom I salute, make our senses do good. May our lives be without any hindrance.

ARGHYA-PRADANAM

अर्घ्यप्रदानम्

ओं भूर्भुवस्सुवः तत् सवितुर्वरेण्यं भर्गो देवस्य धीमहि । धियो यो नः प्रचोदयात् ॥

Om bhurbhuvassuvah | Tat Saviturvarenyam bhargo devasya dhimahi | dhiyo yo nah prachodayaat ||

With this mantra, before sunrise take water filling both hands and pour thrice to the East. At noon, you must stand facing north and pour water twice. At night before sunset in a sitting posture, the thumb should be apart when offering the अर्घ्यं (arghya).

PRAYASCHITTARGHYAM

प्रायश्चित्तार्घ्यम्

प्राणायामः ॥ ओं भूः + भूर्भुवस्सुवरोम् ॥ अर्घ्यम् । ओं भूर्भुवस्सुवः + धियो यो नः प्रचोदयात् ॥ ओं भूर्भुवस्सुवः ॥

Pranayamamah || Om bhuh + bhurbhuvassuvarom || Arghyam | Om bhurbhuvassuvah + dhiyo yo nah prachodayaat || Om bhurbhuvassuvah ||

Then *Pranayama* should be done and then the प्रायश्चित्तार्घ्यं *Prayaschittarghya* must be poured afterwards uttering ओं भूर्भुवस्सुवः *Om bhurbhuvassuvah.* Circumambulate the head with water.

AIKYANUSANDHAANAM

ऐक्यानुसन्धानम्

असावादित्यो ब्रह्म । ब्रह्मैवास्मि ॥

Asavadityo Brahma | Brahmaivaasmi ||

With the two hands touch the breast, close the eyes and deeply meditate on the truth that the *Jeevatman* and *Paramatman* are one.

Meaning

असौ	*Asau*	— This
आदित्यः	*Adityah*	— Sun

ब्रह्म	*Brahma*	—	Is Brahma
अहं	*Aham*	—	I also
ब्रह्मैव	*Brahmaiva*	—	Verily Brahman
अस्मि	*Asmi*	—	Am

Do *Achamanam* after that

DEVA-TARPANAM

देव-तर्पणम्

आदित्यं तर्पयामि । सोमं तर्पयामि । अंगारकं तर्पयामि । बुधं तर्पयामि । बृहस्पतिं तर्पयामि । शुक्रं तर्पयामि । शनैश्चरं तर्पयामि । राहुं तर्पयामि । केतुं तर्पयामि ।

केशवं तर्पयामि । नारायणं तर्पयामि । माधवं तर्पयामि । गोविन्दं तर्पयामि । विष्णुं तर्पयामि । मधुसूदनं तर्पयामि । त्रिविक्रमं तर्पयामि । वामनं तर्पयामि । श्रीधरं तर्पयामि । हृषीकेशं तर्पयामि । पद्मनाभं तर्पयामि । दामोदरं तर्पयामि ।

Adityam tarpayami / Somam tarpayami / Angarakam tarpayami / Budham tarpayami / Brihaspatim tarpayami / Sukram tarpayami / Sanaischaram tarpayami / Rahum tarpayami / Ketum tarpayami //

Kesavam tarpayami / Narayanam tarpayami / Madhavam tarpayami / Govindam tarpayami / Vishnum tarpayami / Madhusoodanam tarpayami / Trivikramam tarpayami / Vamanam tarpayami / Sreedharam tarpayami / Hrishikesam tarpayami Damodaram tarpayami //

Sitting facing the East in the morning and noon and facing the North in the evening, we should pour water. It should not be poured as a current.

Meaning

आदित्यं	*Adityam*	—	The Sun
सोमं	*Somam*	—	The Moon
अंगारकं	*Angarakam*	—	Mars
बुधं	*Budham*	—	Mercury
बृहस्पतिं	*Brihaspatim*	—	Jupiter
शुक्रं	*Sukram*	—	Venus
शनैश्चरं	*Sanaischaram*	—	Saturn
राहुं	*Rahum*	—	Rahu
केतुं	*Ketum*	—	Ketu
तर्पयामि	*Tarpayami*	—	I propitiate.

From Kesava upto Damodara, the twelve names of Lord Vishnu are the tutelary deities of the twelve months of the year beginning with *Dhanus.* Then with the *Achamanam* the preliminary part of Sandhya Vandanam is over.

Now comes the second part, beginning with the Japa-Sankalpa.

SANDHYA-VANDANA JAPAARAMBHAH

सन्ध्यावन्दनजपारम्भः

संकल्पः ॥

शुक्लाम्बरधरं विष्णुं शशिवर्णं चतुर्भुजम् ।
प्रसन्नवदनं ध्यायेत् सर्वविघ्नोप-शान्तये ॥

ओं भूः + भूर्भुवस्सुवरोम् । (प्राणायामः) ॥

ममोपात्त-समस्त-दुरितक्षय-द्वारा श्रीपरमेश्वरप्रीत्यर्थं प्रातः सन्ध्या-गायत्री-महामंत्र-जपं करिष्ये ॥

(माध्यान्हिके-गायत्री-महामंत्र-जपं करिष्ये। सायं सन्ध्या-गायत्री-महामंत्र-जपं करिष्ये।) ॥

Suklambaradharam Vishnum sasivarnam chaturbhujam /

Prasannavadanam dhyayet sarvavighnopa-santhaye //

Om bhu+Bhurbhuvassuvarom // (*Pranayamah*) //

Mamopatta-samasta-duritakshayadwara Sriparameswara-preetyartham Pratah Sandhya – Gayatri – Mahamantra -japam karishye /

Madhyanhika-Gayatri-Mahamantra-Japam-Karishye / *Sayam Sandhya - Gayatri - Mahamantra - japam karishye* /

This should be done sitting on a seat with the eyes half closed and not seeing anything external. The water vessel must be placed in front, facing the East in the morning, and North at noon and the West in the evening.

Gayatri - Maha - Mantra -Japam karishye - I shall do the japa of the great mantra Gayatri.

Afterwards comes the *Pranava Japa* and the *Pranayama*.

प्रणवस्य ऋषिर्ब्रह्म देवी-गायत्री छन्दः परमात्मा देवता ॥

Pranavasya Rishirbhahma, Devi-Gayatri Chhandah, Paramatma Devata //

भूरादि-सप्त-व्याहृतीनां अत्रि-भृगु-कुत्स-वसिष्ठ-गौतम-काश्यप-आंगिरस ऋषयः ॥ गायत्री उष्णिक्-अनुष्टुप् बृहती पंक्ती-त्रिष्टुप् जगती छन्दांसि ॥ अग्नि-वायु-अर्क-वागीश-वरुण-इन्द्र-विश्वेदेवा देवताः ॥

Bhuradi sapta vyahriteenam Atri-Brigu-Kutsa-Vasishtha-Gautama-Kashyapa-Angirasa-rishayah / / Gayatri Ushnik - Anushtup Brihati Pangthi - Thrishtup - Jagati Chhandamsi // Agni-Vayu-Arka-Vageesa Varuna-Indra-Viswedeva Devatah //

When naming the rishi, the head, when naming the chhandas, the mouth and when naming the devata the breast should be touched by the right hand.

As described before, one *pranayama* needs the *japam* of the mantra thrice, at least three *pranayama* must be done. Those who are not able to practise *Puraka*, *Kumbhakas* and *Rechaka*, should repeat the mantra ten times.

ओं भूः । ओं भुवः । ओं सुवः । ओं महः । ओं जनः । ओं तपः । ओं सत्यं ।। ओं तत् सवितुर्वरेण्यं भर्गो देवस्य धीमहि । धियो यो नः प्रचोदयात।

ओमापो ज्योती रसोऽमृतं ब्रह्म भूर्भुवस्सुवरोम् ।।

Om Bhuh / Om Bhuvah // Om Suvah / Om Mahah / Om Janah / Om Tapah / Om Satyam / Om Tat Saviturvarenyam Bhargo Devasysa Dhimahi / Dhiyo Yo Nah Prachodayaat / Omapo Jyotirasomritam Brahma Bhurbhuvassuvarom //

GAYATRI AVAHANAM

गायत्री-आवाहनम्

आयात्वित्यनुवाकस्य वामदेव ऋषिः । अनुष्टुप् छन्दः गायत्री देवता ।।

आयातु वरदा देवि अक्षरं ब्रह्मसंमितम् । गायत्रि छन्दसां मातरिदं ब्रह्म जुषस्व नः ।। ओजोसि सहोसि बलमसि भ्राजोसि देवानां धाम नामासि विश्वमसि विश्वायुः सर्वमसि सर्वायु-रभिभूरों गायत्रीमावाहयामि सावित्रीमावाहयामि सरस्वतीमावाहयामि ।।

Aayatwityanuvakasya Vamadeva Rishih / Anushtup Chhandah / Gayatri Devata /

Aayaatu Varada Devi Aksharam Brahmasammitam / Gayatri Chhandasam Mataridam Brahma Jushaswa Nah / Ojosi Sahosi Balamasi Bhrajosi Devanam Dhama Namasi Viswamasi Viswayuh Sarvamasi Sarvayu-rabhibhoorom Gayatri mavahayami Savitrimavahayami Saraswatimavahayami //

Reciting this mantra, the Gayatri Devi should be thought of as manifesting in the lotus of the heart. With the sign of invocation, the hands should be turned inwards in front of the heart.

GAYATRI NYASAH

गायत्री न्यासः

सावित्र्या ऋषिर्विश्वामित्रः निचृद्गायत्री छन्दः । सविता देवता ॥

Savitriya Rishirvishwamitrah / Nichrudgayatri Chhandah/ Savita Devata //.

Meaning

सावित्र्याः	*Savitriyah* —	Of the Savitri mantra (i. e. the Gayatri mantra)
ऋषि-विश्वामित्रः	*Rishirvishwamitrah* —	Vishwamitra is the Rishi
निचृद्गायत्री छन्दः	*Nichrugayatri Chhandah*—	The Nichrud Gayatri is the metre.
सविता देवता	*Savita Devata* —	And Sun is the deity.
ओं	*Om*	
भूर्भुवस्सुवः	*Bhurbhuvassuvah*	

तत्सवितुर्वरेण्यं — *Tatsaviturvarenyam*
भर्गो देवस्य — *Bhargo Devasya*
धीमहि — *Dhimahi*
धियो यो नः — *Dhiyo Yo Nah*
प्रचोदयात् — *Prachodayat*

The Gayatri Japa must be done standing facing the East in the morning and at noon, and sitting facing the West in the evening. At each time the *japam* should be done repeating the mantra 108 times. If there be no time to do so many times, it should be done at least 54 or 28 times. The *japam* must be done with the thumb touching the second line of second finger and then in the third line of that finger. Then the three lines of the little finger should be touched beginning from bottom to top, afterwards the top lines of the second and middle fingers should be touched and then the three lines from top to bottom of the fore-finger should be touched. A rudraksha or tulsi mala may be used for the japa.

GAYATRI—UPASTHANAM
गायत्री उपस्थानम्

प्राणायामः ।। प्रातः सन्ध्या, (आदित्य), (सायं सन्ध्या), उपस्थानं करिष्ये ।।

उत्तमे शिखरे देवि भूम्यां पर्वतमूर्धनि ।
ब्राह्मणेभ्यो ह्यनुज्ञानं गच्छ देवि यथा सुखम् ।।

Pranayamah / / Praatah Sandhya, (Aditya), (Saayam Sandhya) Upasthanam karishye // Uttame shikhare devi bhoomyaam parvata-moordhani / Brahmanebhyo hyanujnaanam gachha devi yathaa sukham //

After the *japam* of *Gayatri*, the prayer to that deity to go to her own place is called *Gayatri Upasthanam.* First of all the *Pranayama* must be done.

प्रातः सन्ध्या उपस्थानं करिष्ये *Praatah Sandhya Upasthanam Karishye*

I do the upasthanam (of Gayatri) in the morning. In the noon; it is said आदित्य उपस्थानं करिष्ये *Aditya upasthanam Karishye* i. e. I do the upasthanam of *Aditya*. In the evening it is said :' सायं सन्ध्या उपस्थानं करिष्ये *Saayam Sandhya Upasthanam Karishye.* i. e. I do the upasthanam of the evening *Sandhya.*

Meaning

देवि	*Devi*	— O Shining Gayatri Devi !
भूम्याम्	*Bhoomyaam*	— In the earth
ब्राह्मणेभ्यः	*Brahmanebhyah*	— To us who do the worship of Brahman.
अनुज्ञानं	*Anujnanam*	— Blessing.
पर्वत-मूर्धनि	*Parvata-moordhani*	— On the top of Mount Meru
उत्तमे शिखरे	*Uttame shikhare*	— In the excellent peak which is your abode.
यथा सुखम्	*Yathaa sukham*	— Happily
गच्छ	*Gachha*	— Please go

O resplendent Goddess of Gayatri ! blessing us of the earth, who do the worship of the Brahman, please be seated happily in your abode on the excellent peak above Mount Meru.

SURYA UPASTHANAM

सूर्य उपस्थानम्

मित्रस्य चर्षणी धृतः श्रवो देवस्य सानसिम् । सत्यं चित्रश्रवस्तमम् ।

मित्रो जनान् यातयति प्रजानन् मित्रो दाधार पृथिवी-मुत द्याम् । मित्रः कृष्टी-रनिमिषाभिचष्टे सत्याय हव्यं घृतवद्विधेम ॥

प्र स मित्र मर्तो अस्तु पयस्वान् यस्त आदित्य शिक्षति व्रतेन । न हन्यते न जीयते त्वोतो नैनमंहो अश्नोत्यन्तितो न दूरात् ॥

Mitrasya charshani dhritah sravo devasya saanasim / Satyam chitrasravastamam //

Mitro janan yaatayati prajaanan Mitro daadhaara Prithiveemutadyaam / Mitrah krishtee - ranimishaabhichashte Satyaaya havyam ghritavadvidhema //

Pra Sa Mitra Marto Astu Payaswaan Yasta Aditya Sikshati Vratena / Na Hanyate Na Jeeyate Twoto Nainama-gumho Asnotyantito Na Dooraat //

After *japam* fold your hands and stand facing the East; then worship the Paramatma inside the Solar Orb with the following mantra :—

Meaning

चर्षणी धृतः *Charshanee dhritah*	—	Protecting the subjects
मित्रस्य देवस्य *Mitrasya Devasya*	—	Of the Sun God
सानसिम् *Saanasim*	—	Worthy of being Worshipped
सत्यम् *Satyam*	—	Permanent

चित्रश्रवस्तमम् *Chitrasrava-stamam* —	Excelling in attracting the minds of heavens.
श्रवः *Sravah* —	Fame and Greatness (I meditate on)
मित्रः *Mitrah* —	Sun
प्रजानन् *Prajaanan* —	All knowing
जनान् *Janaan* —	People
यातयति *Yaatayati* —	Guides
मित्रः *Mitrah* —	Sun
पृथिवीम् *Prithiveem* —	Earth
उत *Uta* —	And also
द्याम् *Dyaam* —	The Sky
दाधार *Daadhaara* —	Supports
मित्रः *Mitrah* —	Sun
कृष्टीः *Krishteeh* —	Beings
अनिमिषा *Animishaa* —	Without closing the eyes
अभिचष्टे *Abhichashte* —	Sees
सत्याय *Satyaaya* —	To get permanent results.
घृतवद् हव्यम् *Ghrita Vad Havyam* —	The offering with ghee
विधेम *Vidhema* —	We give
मित्र आदित्य *Mitra Aditya* —	O God Sun, who is also called Mitra
यः *Yah* —	He Who
व्रतेन *Vratena* —	With regularity
ते *Te* —	You
शिक्षति *Sikshati* —	Desires to worship
स मर्त्यः *Sa Martyah* —	That man
प्रयस्वान् *Payaswaan* —	With the full effect of dharma
अस्तु *Astu* —	May become
त्वा उतः *Twaa Utah* —	The man protected by you

न हन्यते *Na Hanyate* — Will not suffer by disease
न जीयते *Na jeeyate* — Will not die before hundred
एनम् *Enam* — This man
अंन्ह *Agumhah* — Sin
अन्तित: *Antitah* — Near
दूरात् *Dooraat* — Far
न अश्नोति *Na Asnoti* — Does not suffer

I meditate on the fame and greatness of that excellent attracter of the minds of heavens which never perishes. who worship the Sun God who protects all subjects.

The Sun is all-knowing and guides people. That God supports earth and heaven. He looks vigilantly with unclosed eyes all beings. I offer oblation full of ghee to get imperishable results. O Sun, friend of Universe, he who with regularity desires to worship you, may that mortal get the perfect fruit of dharma. He, who is protected by you, will not suffer from any disease; he will live a hundred years; sin from near or far will not torment him.

MADHYANHE

मध्याह्ने

आ सत्येन रजसा वर्तमानो निवेशयन्नमृतं मर्त्यं च। हिरण्ययेन सविता रथेनाऽऽदेवो याति भुवना विपश्यन् ॥

उद्वयं तमसस्परि पश्यन्तो ज्योतिरुत्तरम्। देवं देवत्रा सूयमगन्म ज्योतिरुत्तमम्। उदुत्यं जातवेदसं देवं वहन्ति केतवः दृशे विश्वाय सूर्यम् ॥

चित्रं देवाना-मुदगा-दनीकं चक्षु-मित्रस्य वरुणस्याग्नेः। आ प्रा द्यावा पृथिवी अन्तरिक्षं सूर्य आत्मा जगत-स्तस्थुषश्च। तच्चक्षु-र्देवहितं पुरस्ता-च्छुक्र-मुच्चरत् ॥

पश्येम शरदश्शतं, जीवेम शरदश्शतं, नन्दाम शरदश्शतं, मोदाम शरदश्शतं, भवाम शरदश्शतं, शृणवाम शरदश्शतं, प्रब्रवाम शरदश्शतं, अजीताः स्याम शरदश्शतं, ज्योक् च सूर्यं दृशे ॥

य उदगान्महतोऽर्णवात् विभ्राजमानः सरिरस्य मध्यात् स मा वृषभो लोहिताक्षस्सूर्यो विपश्चिन् मनसा पुनातु ॥

Aasatyena rajasa vartamano nivesayannamritam martyam cha| Hiranyayena Savita rathenaadevo yaati bhuvana vipasyan || Udvayam tamasaspari pasyanto jyotiruttaram| Devam Devatraa Suryamaganma jyotiruttamam |

Udutyam Jatavedasam Devam vahanti ketavah| Drise viswaaya Suryam || Chitramdevana-mudagadaneekam chakshurmitrasya varunasyyagneh | Aa praa dyavaa prithivee anthariksha-gum Surya Atma Jagata-stasthushascha | Tachchakshurdevahitam purasthacchukra muchcharat ||

Pasyema saradassatam, Jeevema saradassatam, Nandaama Saradassatam, Modama saradassatam, bhavama saradassatagum-srunavama saradassatam, prabravama saradassatamajeetasyama saradassatam, jyokcha Suryam drise.||

Ya udagaanmahatornavaad vibhrajamanah sarirasya madhyaat sama vrishabho lohitaakshassuryo vipaschin manasa punatu ||

Meaning :

सत्येन *Satyena*	—	By the light of the Self
रजसा *Rajasa*	—	By the light seen by the eyes
अमृतं मर्त्यं च *Amritam martyam cha*	—	The Gods and mortals

निवेशायन्	*Nivcsayan*	Putting them in their work
आवर्तमानः	*Aa vartamanah*	Coming round
सविता देवः	*Savita Devah*	The Sun God
हिरण्ययेन	*Hiranyayena*	The golden
रथेन	*Rathena*	By chariot
भुवनाः	*Bhuvanah*	Worlds
विपश्यन्	*Vipasyan*	Seeing particularly
याति	*Yaati*	Travels.

The Sun God who secs by the light of the soul and by the light of eyes the Gods and mortals and engaging them in their respective works, goes round in the golden chariot and tiavels with a particular eyc looking at the world.

उद् तमसस्परि	*Ud Tamas-aspari*	He who rises swallowing the darkness
उत्तरं ज्योतिः	*Uttaram Jyotih*	The excellent Light
देवत्राः	*Devatrah*	The protector of even the Gods
देवं सूर्यम्	*Devam Suryam*	The Sun God
पश्यन्तः	*Pasyantah*	The Seers
वयम्	*Vayam*	We
उत्तमं ज्योतिः	*Uttamam Jyotih*	The excellent light of the soul
अगन्म	*Aganma*	May we attain

May we attain the excellent light of the Soul, we who see the Sun God who has a higt form of light and rises swallowing darkness and the protector of even the Gods.

त्यं *Tyam*	— That famous
जातवेदसं देवं *Jatavedasam Devam*	— The all erasing God
सूर्यम् *Suryam*	— The Sun
केतवः *Ketavah*	— Rays
उद्वहन्ति *Udvahanti*	— Is borne

That famous, all knowing Sun God, is borne by the rays, his horses.

मित्रस्य वरुणस्य अग्नेः *Mitrasya Varunasya Agneh*	— To Mitra, Varuna and Agni
चक्षुः *Chakshuh*	— Like an eye
देवानां चित्रं अनीकं *Devanaam Chitram Aneekam*	— The Sun who is the form of all Gods.
जगतस्तस्थुषश्च *Jagatas-tasthushascha*	— The movable and the im-movable
आत्मा *Atma*	— The Soul
सूर्यः *Suryah*	— The Sun
द्यावा पृथिवीम् अन्तरिक्षं *Dyaavaa Prithiveem Antariksham*	— The Heaven, the Earth and the atmosphere
आ प्राः *Aa Prah*	— Pervades in the East rising
पुरस्तात् शुक्रं उच्चरत् *Purasthat sukram uchcharat*	— via pure state
देवहितं चक्षुः *Devahitam chakshuh*	— Like an eye doing good to the Gods.
तत् *Tat*	— That Solar Orb.
शरदश्शतं *Saradassatam*	— A hundred years.
पश्येम *Pasyema*	— May we see and submit ourselves
जीवेम शरदश्शतं *Jeevema saradassatam*	— May we live thus a hundred years.

नन्दाम शरदश्शतम् *Nandaama saradassatam*	—	May we rejoice with our people a hundred years.
मोदाम शरदश्शतं *Modaama saradassatam*	—	May we be joyous for a hundred years.
भवाम शरदश्शत *Bhavaama saradassatam*	—	May we shine with fame for a hundred years.
शृणवाम शरदश्शतं *Srunavaama saradassatam*	—	May we hear pleasant things for a hundred years.
प्रब्रवाम शरदश्शतं *Prabravaama saradassatam*	—	May we speak good things for a hundred years.
अजीताः स्याम शरदश्शतम *Ajeetah Syama saradassatam*	—	May we be not overcome by bad defeat for a hundred years.
ज्योक् च *Jyok cha*	—	Thus for a long time
सूर्यं *Suryam*	—	The Sun
दृशे *Drise*	—	May we realise.

May the Sun who is an eye to Mitra, Varuna and Agni, the embodiment of various Gods, rise high. The Sun God, the Soul of moving and unmoving pervades the earth, the heaven and the atmosphere. May we see and bow for hundred years. That Sun who does good like the eye to the Gods, the pure light that rises in the east. Let us mix in joy for a hundred years with our own people. May we be happy for a hundred years. May we be bright with good fame for a hundred years. May we hear pleasant things for a hundred years. May we speak good things for a hundred years. May we not be soiled by bad defeat for a hundred years. May we see the Sun God for such a long time.

वृषभः *Vrishabhah*	He who confers or grants the desired results

लोहिताक्षः	*Lohitakshah*	—	The red eyed one
विपश्चित्	*Vipaschit*	—	The all knowing
यः	*Yah*	—	He
विभ्राजमानः	*Vibhrajumanah*	—	Shining everywhere
महत् अर्णवात्	*Mahat Arnavaat*	—	The great ocean
सरिरस्य मध्यात्	*Sarirasya Madhyaat*	—	From the middle of water
उदगात्	*Udaguat*	—	Rises in the morning
सूर्यः	*Suryah*	—	That Sun God
मा	*Maa*	—	Me
मनसा	*Manasaa*	—	With the whole mind
पुनातु	*Punatu*	—	Purify.

May the fulfiller of desired results, the red-eyed, all-knowing, shining everywhere, rising from the midst of the water, may that Sun God purify me with all my mind.

सायंकाले

Sayankale : (Evening)

इमं मे वरुण श्रुधी हवमद्या च मृडय। त्वामवस्युराचके। तत्वा यामि ब्रह्मणा वन्दमानस्तदाशास्ते यजमानो हविर्भिः। अहेडमानो वरुणेह बोध्युरुशं स मा न आयुः प्रमोषीः॥ यच्चिद्धि ते विशो यथा प्र देव वरुण व्रतम्। मिनीमसि द्यविद्यवि॥

यत् किञ्चेदं वरुण दैव्ये जनेऽभिद्रोहं मनुष्याश्चरामसि। अचित्ती यत्तव धर्मा युयोपिम मा नस्तस्मादेनसो देव रीरिषः। कितवासो यद्रिरिपुर्न दीवी यद्वा घा सत्यमुत यन्न विद्म। सर्वा ता विष्य शिथिरेव देवाथा ते स्याम वरुण प्रियासः॥

Imam me Varuna srudhee havamadyaa cha mridaya / Tvaamavasyuraachake // Tatvaa yaami brahmanaa vandamaanasta-

daasaaste yajamaano havirbhih | Ahedamaano Varuneha Bodhyurusagumsa maa na Aayuh pramosheeh || yatchiddhi te visho yathaa pradeva Varuna Vratam | Mineemasi dyavidyavi || Yat kinchedam Varuna daivye janebhidroham manushyaascharaamasi | Achittee yattava dharmaa yuyopima maa nastasmaadenaso Deva reerishah || kitavaaso yadriripurna deevi yadvaa ghaa satyamuta yanna vidma | sarvaa taa vishya shithireva devaatha te syaama Varuna priyaasah ||

Meaning

वरुण *Varuna*	—	O Varuna
मे *Me*	—	My
इमं *Imam*	—	This
हवं *Havam*	—	Supplication, request
श्रुधी *Srudhee*	—	Hear
अद्या च *Adyaa cha*	—	Even now
मृडय *Mridaya*	—	Be loving
अवस्युः *Avasyuh*	—	Desiring protection
त्वां *Tvaam*	—	You
आचके *Aachake*	—	I pray

O God Varuna ! Hear my prayer. Be gracious even now. I pray to you seeking protection.

ब्रह्मणा *Brahmanaa*	—	By the Vedic mantras
वन्दमानः *Vandamaanah*	—	Praying
तत् *Tat*	—	For that
त्वां *Tvaa*	—	You
यामि *Yaami*	—	I take refuge
यजमानः *Yajamaanah*	—	The sacrificer
हविर्भिः *Havirbhih*	—	With offerings
तत् *Tat*	—	That

आशास्ते *Aasaaste*	—	I desire
उरुशँ्स वरुण *Urusagumsa Varuna*	—	O renowned Varuna
अहेडमानः *Ahedamaanah*	—	Not slighting
इह *Iha*	—	Now
बोधि *Bodhi*	—	You must fulfil my prayer
नः *Nah*	—	Our
आयुः *Aayuh*	—	Life
मा प्रमोषीः *Maa pramosheeh*	—	Do not lessen.

I take refuge in You praising with Vedic mantras. The sacrificer desires that only by his offerings. "O famous Varuna! not slighting fulfil my prayer even now. Do not decrease our life periods."

यद् चित् *Yad Chit*	—	Ho
देव वरुण *Deva Varuna*	—	O God Varuna
विशः यथा *Visah Yatha*	—	Like the people without discrimination
ते व्रतं *Te vratam*	—	Your worship
द्यवि द्यवि *dyavi dyavi*	—	Every day
प्र मिनीमसि *Pra mineemasi*	—	By carelessness, not doing and giving up
देव वरुण *Deva Varuna*	—	O God Varuna
दैव्ये जने *Daivye Jane*	—	To the hosts of Gods
मनुष्याः *Manushyaah*	—	We men
इदं अभिद्रोहं *Idam abhidroham*	—	This deceit
अचित्ती *Achittee*	—	Unknowingly
यत्किञ्च चरामसि *Yatkincha charaamasi*	—	Whatever I have done

तव *Tava* — Your
धर्मा: *Dharmaah* — Dharma
यत् युयोपिम *Yat yuyopima* — Whatever we spoil
देव *Deva* — O God Varuna
तस्मादेनसा *Tasmadenasa* — By that sin
न: *Nah* — Us
मा रीरिष: *Maa reerishah* — Be gracious without punishing us.

O God Varuna ! Like the indiscriminating people thy regular daily worship might have been omitted by negligence. O God Varuna ! Such deceit might have been done unconsciously. All that we have done, thy dharmas which we have spoiled, O God Varuna ! Save us by not punishing us for that sin.

कितवास: *Kitavaasah* — Like those who play dice
न दीवि *Na deevi* — That which good people do not resort to
यद् *Yad* — That fault wrongly
रिरिपु: *Riripuh* — Has attributed to me
यद्वा घा *Yadvaa ghaa* — Or the sins
सत्यं *Satyam* — Really done
उत: *Utah* — And also
न विद्म *Na vidma* — Have done and yet do not know
यत् *Yat* — That
ता: सर्वा: *Taah Sarvaah* — All those
शिथिरेव *Sithireva* — Just as they would be scattered without any pain

विष्य *Vishya*	—	Destroy
देव वरुण *Deva Varuna*	—	O God Varuna
अथा *Atha*	—	Afterwards
ते *Te*	—	To you
प्रियास: *Priyaasah*	—	Beloved ones
स्याम *Syaama*	—	May we always become.

The blame attributed to me unjustly like the players of dice or the sin which I might have done knowingly and also those which I have done unknowingly, all these may be scattered and destroyed. O God Varuna ! May we afterwards always become beloved of You.

SAMASHTYABHIVAADANAM

समष्ट्यभिवादनम्

सन्ध्यायै नमः । सावित्र्यै नमः गायत्र्यै नमः सरस्वत्यै नमः। सर्वाभ्यो देवताभ्यो नमो नमः ।। कामोऽकार्षीन्मन्युरकार्षीन्नमो नमः ।

Sandhyaayai namah | Saavitryai namah | Gaayatryai namah | Saraswatyai namah | Sarvaabhyo Devataabhyo namo namah || Kamokarsheennmanyurakaarsheennamo namah

After Japam the mantras सन्ध्यायै नमः *Sandhyaayai namah* etc. should be uttered folding the hands beginning with the quarter which one faces at the time of the japam. Finally looking to that very quarter सर्वाभ्यो देवताभ्यो नमः

Sarvaabhyo Devataabhyo namah and कामोऽकार्षीन्मन्युरकार्षीन्नमो नमः *kamokaarsheenmanyurakaarsheennamo namah* should be uttered with folded hands.

Meaning

सन्ध्यायै नमः *Sandhyaayai namah*	—	Prostration to Sandhya Goddess
सावित्र्यै नमः *Saavitryai namah*	—	Prostration to Goddess Savitri
गायत्र्यै नमः *Gaayatryai namah*	—	Prostration to Goddess Gayatri
सरस्वत्यै नमः *Saraswatyai namah*	—	Salutation to Goddess Saraswati
सर्वाभ्यो देवताभ्यो नमो नमः *Sarvaabhyo Devataabhyo namo namah*	—	Salutation again and again to all the deities
कामः अकार्षीत् *Kaamah akaarsheet*	—	Kama (Desire) did it
मन्युः अकार्षीत् *Manyuh akarsheet*	—	The anger did it, i.e. I did not of my own will commit sins. Falling under the control of desire and anger, I did bad things unknowingly. Forgive me.
नमो नमः *Namo Namah*	—	O Gods ! I again and again salute You.

अभिवादये (वैश्वामित्र, अघमर्षण, कौशिक त्रय) आर्षेय प्रवरान्वित, (कौशिक) गोत्रः (आपस्तम्ब) सूत्रः (यजुः) शाखाध्यायी श्री (कृष्ण) शर्मा नामाहं अस्मि भोः ॥

Abhivaadaye (Vaisvaamitra, Aghamarshana, Kausika, Traya) Aarsheya Pravaraanvita, (Kausika) gotrah, Aapastamba Sutrah, (Yajuh) Sakhaaddyaayee Sri (Krishna) Sarma Naamaaham Asmi Bhoh ||

The *Sandhya Devi* should be saluted touching the two ears with two hands uttering this mantra and then touching the feet, the thumbs and the earth.

Meaning

अभिवादये *Abhivaadaye*	—	I salute your lotus feet
वैश्वामित्र *Vaishvaamitra* अघमर्षण *Aghamarshana* कौशिक त्र्यार्षेय प्रवरान्वित *Kausika, Trayaarsheya Pravaraanvita*	}	The heads of the Gotra, the three rishis Vaisvaamitra, Aghamarshana and Kausika
कौशिक गोत्रः *Kausika Gotrah*	—	Born of Kausika gotra
आपस्तम्ब सूत्रः *Aapastamba Sutrah*	—	One who does works according to the *sutras* of *Aapastamba*
यजुः शाखाध्यायी *Yajuh Sakhaaddyaayee*	—	Student of yajurveda
श्री कृष्ण शर्मा नामा *Sri Krishna Sharma Nama* अहं अस्मि *Aham Asmi*	}	I bear the name of Sri Krishna Sarma.

I salute You, the form of all Gods and Goddesses. I belong to the family of which Kausika is the head and Vaisvaamitra, Aghamarshana and Kausika are the three prominent rishis. I follow the Apastamba Sutra in performing vedic rites. I am a student of Yajurveda and my name is Sri Krishna Sarma.

Note: The rishi and gotra varga i. e. the names of the heads of the gotra and the three rishis, the names of the founders of the Sutras and of the Veda Sakha of which the performer of Sandhya Vandana is a student, may vary with individuals. Ed.

DIGDEVATA VANDANAM

दिग्देवता वन्दनम्

प्राच्यै दिशे नमः। दक्षिणायै दिशे नमः। प्रतीच्यै दिशे नमः। उदीच्यै दिशे नमः। ऊर्ध्वाय नमः। अधराय नमः। अन्तरिक्षाय नमः। भूम्यै नमः। ब्रह्मणे नमः। विष्णवे नमः। मृत्यवे नमः॥

Praachyai Dise Namah || Dakshinaayai Dise Namah || Prateechyai Dise Namah || Udeechyai Dise Namah || Oordhwaaya Namah || Adharaaya Namah || Antarikshaaya Namah || Bhoomyai Namah || Brahmane Namah || Vishnave Namah || Mrityave Namah ||

Beginning from the quarter facing which the *japa* was done, the four quarters are saluted as well as the upper side and lower side and the middle portion and the Gods of the quarters, and afterwards the earth and the three Gods Brahma, Vishnu and Siva.

Meaning

प्राच्यै दिशे नमः *Praachyai Dise Namah* — Salutations to Eastern side

दक्षिणायै दिशे नमः *Dakshinaayai Dise Namah* — Salutations to South

प्रतीच्यै दिशे नमः *Prateechyai Dise Namah* — Salutations to West

उदीच्यै दिशे नमः *Udeechyai Dise Namah* — Salutations to Gods of the the Northern side.

ऊर्ध्वाय नमः *Oordhwaaya Namah* — Prostrations to the Gods of upper world.

अधराय नमः *Adharaaya Namah* — Salutations to the Gods of lower worlds.

अन्तरिक्षाय नमः *Antarikshaaya Namah* — Salutations to Gods of middle World.

भूम्यै नमः *Bhoomyai Namah* — Salutations to the Goddess Earth.

ब्रह्मणे नमः *Brahmane Namah* — Salutations to Brahma.

विष्णवे नमः *Vishnave Namah* — Salutations to Vishnu.

मृत्यवे नमः *Mrityaye Namah* — Salutations to Rudra.

Salutations to Gods of East, South, West and North, as well as to those who are in the upper world, the lower world and the mid-world. Salutations to Earth. Salutations to Brahma, Vishnu and Rudra.

YAMAVANDANAM

यमवन्दनम्

यमाय नमः। यमाय धर्मराजाय मृत्यवे चान्तकाय च। वैवस्वताय कालाय सर्वभूतक्षयाय च।

औदुम्बराय दध्नाय नीलाय परमेष्ठिने। वृकोदराय चित्राय चित्रगुप्ताय वै नमः॥

चित्रगुप्ताय वै नम ओं नम इति।

Yamaaya Namah |! Yamaaya Dharmaraajaaya Mrityave Chhantakaaya cha || Vaivaswataaya Kaalaaya Sarvabhoota-kshayaaya cha ||

Oudumbaraaya Dadhnaaya Neelaaya parameshtine || Vrikodaraaya Chitraaya Chitraguptaaya Vai Namah || Chitraguptaaya Vai Nama Om Nama Iti ||.

This mantra should be uttered facing the South.

Meaning

यमाय नमः *Yamaaya Namah*	—	Salutations to Yama.
यमाय *Yamaaya*	—	One who controls all.
धर्मराजाय *Dharmaraajaya*	—	The God Dharma.
मृत्यवे च *Mrityave cha*	—	And the God who destroys
अन्तकाय च *Antakaaya cha*	—	And the God who makes an end.
वैवस्वताय *Vaivaswataaya*	—	The Son of the Sun.
कालाय *Kaalaaya*	—	The personification of Time
सर्वभूतक्षयाय च *Sarvabhoota-kshayaaya cha*	—	The destroyer of all beings

औदुम्बराय *Oudumbaraaya* — The very strong.

दध्नाय *Dadhnaaya* — The God who is called *Dadhna*

नीलाय *Neelaaya* — Of blue colour.

परमेष्ठिने *Parameshtine* — Worshipped by all.

वृकोदराय *Vrikodaraaya* — Having a big belly.

चित्राय *Chitraaya* — Strange.

चित्रगुप्ताय वै नमः *Chitraguptaaya Namah* — Salutations to Yamadharma raja who keeps his wonderful secrets.

चित्रगुप्ताय वै नम ओं नम इति *Chitraguptaaya Vai Namah Om Nama Iti* — Again salutations to Chitragupta Om Salutations.

Salutations to Yama, Salutations to Him who controls all, King Dharma, the destroyer and end of all, the son of Sun God, the embodiment of Time, the destroyer of all beings, the very strong one who has got the name of *Dadhna*, the blue-bodied, worshipped of all, having a big belly, the strange one who guards these strange secrets. Salutations to that *Yamadharmaraja.* Salutations again to that *Chitragupta.* Salutations to *Om.*

HARIVANDANAM

हरिवन्दनम

ऋतं सत्यं परं ब्रह्म पुरुषं कृष्णपिङ्गलम् । ऊर्ध्वरेतं विरूपाक्षं विश्वरूपाय वै नमो नमः ।। विश्वरूपाय वै नमो नम ओं नम इति ।।

Ritagum Satyam Param Brahma Purusham Krishna-pingalam || Oorddhwaretam Viroopaksham ViswaroopayaVai Namo Namah || Viswaroopaaya Vai Namo Nama Om Nama Iti ||

Facing the north and standing with folded hands this *mantra* should be uttered.

Meaning

ऋतं *Ritagum*	—	The beauty in things seen
सत्यं *Satyam*	—	The basis of sight.
परं ब्रह्म *Param Brahma*	—	Para Brahma (Supreme Being)
पुरुषं *Purusham*	—	Dwelling in all bodies.
कृष्ण-पिङ्गलं *Krishna-Pingalam*	—	The dark Lord Krishna and the red Shiva united as Harihar
ऊर्ध्वरेतं *Oordhwaretam*	—	Whose strength is upwards.
विश्वरूपाय वै *Viswaroopaaya Vai*	—	To that who is the form of the Universe or who assumes all forms.
नमो नमः *Namo Namah*	—	Salutations.
विरूपाक्षं *Viroopaaksham*	—	Three-eyed One.
विश्वरूपाय वै नमो नम ओम्नम इति *Viswaroopaya Vai Namo Nama Om nama Iti*	—	Salutations to Him who assumes all forms. *Om* Salutations.

Salutations to Him who assumes all forms, the beauty of all things seen, the basis of all sights, the *Parabrahma*, the dark-hued *Vishnu* and the red *Shiva* in one, the pure One and the three-eyed One. Salutations to Him Who assumes all forms. *Om* Salutations.

SURYANARAYANA VANDANAM

सूर्यनारायणवन्दनम्

नमः सवित्रे जगदेकचक्षुषे जगत्प्रसूतिस्थितिनाशहेतवे ।
त्रयीमयाय त्रिगुणात्मधारिणे विरिञ्चिनारायणशङ्करात्मने ॥
ध्येयः सदा सवितृमण्डलमध्यवर्ती नारायणः सरसिजासनसन्निविष्टः ।
केयूरवान् मकरकुण्डलवान् किरीटी हारी हिरण्मयवपुर्धृतशङ्खचक्रः ॥
शङ्खचक्रगदापाणे द्वारकानिलयाच्युत । गोविन्द पुण्डरीकाक्ष रक्ष मां शरणागतम् ॥
आकाशात् पतितं तोयं यथा गच्छति सागरम् ॥
सर्वदेवनमस्कारः केशवं प्रति गच्छति ॥ श्रीकेशवं प्रति गच्छत्यों नम इति ।
अभिवादये + अस्मि भोः ॥ (नमस्कारः)

Namah Savitre Jagadeka Chakshushe Jagat-prasooti-sthiti-naasa-hetave, trayee mayaaya trigunaatma-dhaarine Virinchi Naaraayana-Sankaraatmane, Dhyeyah Sadaa Savitrumandala-madhyavartee Naarayanah Sarasijaasana-Samnivishtah ||

Keyuravan Makarakundalavaan Kiritee Haaree Hiranmaya-vapur-dhritha sankha-chakrah. Sankha-Chakra-Gadaapaane Dwarakaanilayaachyuta || Govinda Pundareekaaksha Raksha Maam saranagatam ||

Aakaasaat patitam toyam yatha gacchati saagaram ||

Sarvadeva namaskarah kesavam prati gachchati ||

Sreekesavam prati gacchatyon nama iti || abhivaadaye ....Asmi Bhoh ||

(*Namaskaarah*)

This *mantra* should be uttered facing the quarter in which the *japa* was done, meditating on the Supreme Self Who has taken the forms of three deities, and prostrating.

Meaning

जगदेकचक्षुषे *Jagadeka-chakshushe*	—	The one eye of the universe
जगत्प्रसूतिस्थितिनाशहेतवे *Jagat prasooti-sthiti-naasahetuve*	—	The cause of Creation, maintenance and destruction of the universe.
त्रयीमयाय *Trayee mayaaya*	—	The embodiment of the Vedas.
त्रिगुणात्मधारिणे. विरिञ्चिनारायणशङ्करात्मने *Trigunaatma Dhaarine Virinchi Narayana Sankaraatmane*	—	The three gunas taking the three forms as Brahma, Vishnu and Shiva.
सवित्रे *Savitre*	—	To the Sun God.
नमः *Namah*	—	Salutations.

Salutations to the Sun God, the Eye of the Universe, the Cause of Creation, Maintenance and Destruction of the Universe, the three *Gunas*, taking form as *Brahma*, *Vishnu* and *Shiva*.

सवितृमण्डलमध्यवर्ती *Savitru-mandala-Madhyavartee*	—	He who lives in the centre of the Solar orb
सरसिजासनसन्निविष्टः *Sarasijaasana Sannivishtah*	—	Who sits in *Padmaasana*

केयूरवान् मकरकुण्डलवान् किरीटी हारी *Keyuravaan Makara-kundalavaan Kireetee Haaree* — Who has the bracelets, the big ear-rings in the ear, the crown on the head and the pearl garland dangiing on the breast.

धृतशङ्खचक्रः *Dhrita-Sankha-Chakrah* — Holder of Conch and Discus

हिरण्मयवपुः *Hiranmayavapuh* — Golden-hued body.

नारायणः *Narayanah* — Narayana

सदा ध्येयः *Sadaa Dhyeyah* — Always to be meditated.

Narayana, always to be meditated, sits in Padmaasana in the centre of the Solar orb, has got bracelets on the arms, big ear rings on the ear, crown on the head and a garland of pearl dangling on the breast. He holds the Conch and Discus and is golden-hued in body.

शङ्खचक्रगदापाणे *Sankha-Chakra-Gadaa-Pane* — Thou, Who holdest in the hands the Conch, the Discus and the *Gada* (*mace*)

द्वारका निलयाच्युत *Dwaarkaa* — Dweller of Dwaraka.

Nilaya Achyuta — He who does not lose a particle of his nature.

गोविन्द *Govinda* — Protector of the Earth.

पुण्डरीकाक्ष *Pundareekaaksha* — The lotus-eyed.

शरणागतं मां *Saranaagatam maam* — Me who has taken refuge (in Thee)

रक्ष *Raksha* — Protect.

O holder of the Conch, Discus and *Gada*, the constant dweller in Dwaraka, the indestructible, the protector of the earth, the lotus eyed, save me who has taken refuge in Thee.

आकाशात् *Aukaasaat*	— From the sky
पतितं *Patitam*	— Fallen
तोयं *Toyam*	— Water
सागरम् *Saagaram*	— The ocean.
गच्छति यथा *Gacchati-yathaa*	— Just as it goes.
सर्वदेवनमस्कारः *Sarvadeva-namaskaarah*	— Salutations to all Gods.
केशवं प्रति गच्छति *Kesavam prati gacchati*	— Goes to Kesava.
श्री केशवं प्रति गच्छति ओं नम इति *Sree Kesavam prati gacchati*	— Goes to Sri Kesava
Om Nama iti	— Salutation *Om*.

Just as the waters from the sky go to the Ocean, so salutations to any God reaches Kesava. Om Nama.

SAMARPANAM

समर्पणम्

कायेन वाचा मनसेन्द्रियैर्वा बुध्यात्मना वा प्रकृतेः स्वभावात् ।
करोमि यद्यत् सकलं परस्मै नारायणायेति समर्पयामि ॥

Kaayena Vaacha Manasendriyairvaa Budhyaatmana Vaa Prakriteh Swabhaavaat || Karomi Yadyat Sakalam Parasmai Naraayanaayeti samarpayaami ||.

कायेन *Kaayena*	—	By the body.
वाचा *Vaachaa*	—	By speech.
मनसा *Manasaa*	—	By the mind.
इन्द्रियैर्वा *Indriyairvaa*	—	or by the senses
बुध्यात्मना वा *Budhyaatmana Vaa*	—	or by the intellect
प्रकृतेः स्वभावात् *Prakriteh Swabhaavaat*	—	Or by the character of one's nature.
यद्यद् *Yad Yad*	—	Whatever.
करोमि *Karomi*	—	I do.
सकलं *Sakalam*	—	All that.
परस्मै नारायणाय इति *Parasmai Naraayanaaya iti*	—	To the Supreme God Naraayana
समर्पयामि *Samarpayaami*	—	I dedicate.

I dedicate to Narayana, the Supreme God, whatever I have done by the body, speech, mind, the senses or by the eharacter of nature.

आचमनम् (*Aachamanam*)